YANKEE'S BOOK OF

Whatsits

More than 100 ingenious old-time
indoor and outdoor labor and time savers from
kitchen, barn, shed, and field.

How Many Can You Identify?
Photos, Hints, Answers, and Index

Published MCMLXXV by
YANKEE, INC.
Dublin, New Hampshire
03444

This Book Has Been Prepared by the Staff of Yankee, Inc.
Clarissa M. Silitch, Editor
John B. Pierce, Assistant Editor
Aleta R. Jenks, Designer

Contents

Foreword

To wind up one of his talks about YANKEE Magazine, Editor Judson D. Hale once asked his audience to name the article or feature they liked best in the magazine. Some hesitated, deciding, but one reader's hand shot right up with no delay. "The monthly 'What's It' column," he said.

Hale looked mildly surprised — indeed slightly pained. "But that's an advertisement," he declared, "not YANKEE editorial!"

It is rare that any advertisement draws so much attention as to be considered an editorial feature, but this is what happened with Savogran's intriguing "What's It" campaign, creation of Account Executive James A. Woodburn. Woodburn started hunting for, collecting and writing up whatsits over the Savogran signature back in 1965 with the blessing of the late Clement K. Stodder, company president, whose interest in early American history and artifacts inspired the idea that eventually became the "What's It" series appearing monthly on page 4 of YANKEE Magazine.

Originally, readers were requested to send their guesses directly to the company, which rewarded correct answers with free samples of its products, and great numbers did so. Other enthusiasts, however, addressed their guesses to YANKEE, often including whatsits of their own for identification. Thus YANKEE, without meaning to be at all and before it really knew what was happening, found itself, too, in the whatsit business with the knowledgeable help of its monthly "Oracle," columnist Joseph Chase Allen.

Continuing eager interest in this unique advertising "feature" led Yankee to publish this collection of whatsits as a salute to the many known and unknown craftsmen who invented and shaped, often with only rude tools to help them, these ingenious aids to life in what seems to us a more primitive time than our own, and to those who are dedicated to the preservation of these homely treasures for present and future generations.

We are most grateful to such notable collectors as James A. Keillor of Wading River, N.Y., who has one of the most fabulous collections of "primitives" we have ever seen; Lawrence Cooke of Needham, Mass., who collects a wide variety of household, farm, blacksmith, and cobbler implements and tools; Ralph DeWitt of Wilkes-Barre, Pa., a consistent supplier of the unusual; and Frank Bushey of Bloomfield, Conn., for whatsits from his own collection. Many items are on exhibit at the Old Academy Museum in Wethersfield, Conn., and in the famous Shelburne Museum, Shelburne, Vt. We are indebted also to the many hundreds of YANKEE readers, too numerous to mention in this limited space, who have taken the time and made the effort to offer their "treasures" for use in the series, without recognition or reward, other than the personal satisfaction of seeing their prized possession appear in print.

And finally, we wish to thank the Savogran Company and James A. Woodburn for their generous cooperation in making their material available to Yankee, for their helpful assistance in production of this book, and most of all, for inventing the delightful game of "WHATSITS" in the first place!

Clarissa Silitch, Editor

Guessing WHATSITS
is a fascinating pastime and a great parlor game.
Collecting them can be a lifetime passion!

HOW TO PLAY "WHATSIT?"

Each photo is accompanied by a clue, rhymed or not, to the identity or purpose of the pictured whatsit. Sometimes this will be a multiple choice question; sometimes a rhyme that must be completed with the appropriate word or words — the number of letters in each missing word are usually indicated by blanks. Oft-times a clue will be followed by similar blanks where you fill in the letters with the answer; occasionally a few of the blanks are already filled in as a hint. In other cases, the answer is presented in the form of an anagram, which you must unscramble. In a few places, we have left just a solid line for you to fill in the word or words required, with the number of letters unspecified.

Turn the page to find the answers to each double-page spread. See page 10 for answers to page 62.

Every object pictured, with the exception of the three "mysteries" on page 63, is listed alphabetically in the Index on page 64, along with its number in the book and the page on which it appears. Besides its obvious use as a reference, you will find the Index a helpful aid when inspiration flags, to jog your memory or give you new ideas before resorting to the answers.

In the Kitchen

In the old-time larder, food often appeared in forms quite different from those it takes today. Sugar came in loaves, not boxes; milk came in bottles or great silver milk cans; butter and cheese came in cream and milk, and sausages came in pigs. The shelves held no handy cans of prepared fruit or vegetables or jars of jam or jelly that had not been prepared by the housewife herself. And she had to prepare a lot to tide her over the winter. They ate hearty in those days just to keep warm — no central heating! The warmest room was the kitchen, of course, with the big wood or coal stove that not only did the cooking and baking, but toasted toes and a great many other things to boot. To cope with these conditions of life, the housewife had a whole slew of ingenious gadgets and aids, just as we do now, but hers were as different from ours as her kitchen was. (Can't help thinking, though, that some would come in mighty useful today!) Keep her kitchen in mind as you try to guess these WHATSITS . . .

1) Had Martha Washington
   owned one of these,
   George's pies could have
   been made with ease.

_ _ _ _ _ _ _
_ _ T T _ _ _

Answer for p. 62

124) An early form of Bagatelle.
Assembled, with piece 3) proper-
ly positioned (in reverse of that
shown), this is the game of "Fort",
played with large marbles as
"bowlers" with or without a small
cue stick. Marbles were rolled
into the various pockets of the
game for different scores, for a
winning score of 21 points.

2) If the recipe read diced,
   minced or cubed,
   Chances are that
   this was used.

V _ _ _ T _ _ _ _
_ _ _ P _ _ R

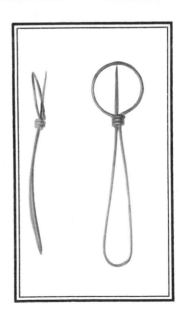

3) Solved a common kitchen
   problem when invented,
   Soggy caps or fingers
   were circumvented.

_ _ _ _ _   _ _ _ _ _ _ opener.

△5) The usefulness of this
device was no idle boast;
Rotated before the fire, it
made great _ _ _ _ _.

△4) Gourmet's gun, it loaded casings for frying, not
firing.

_ _ _ _ _
_ _ _ _ _ F E R

△6) To reduce flavorful
flowers and seeds to the
ground level, you used this:
a) sowing machine; b) flour
mill; c) spice grinder

◁7) Whole hog couldn't
be done;
Made ammunition for the
gourmet's gun.

_ _ _ _
_ _ _ _ _ _ _
(RINDGER)

8) Anyone could put the squeeze on a popular dairy product with this handy C _ _ _ _ _ _ _ _ _ S.

9) Anyone who pines for
   fresh tropical fruits
   Will have a use to which
      this suits.
   What *is* it?

_____

10) Land 'o Lakes, for
    goodness sakes!
  One common form of a
    ubiquitous agitator.

– – – – – –   – – – – –

11) Without this, the cook
   wouldn't have had an edge
          on anything.
          _ N_ _ _ _
_ H_ _ _ _ _ _ _

⇨12) This guillotine-like object served a specific purpose; it is a: a) mouse trap; b) apple slicer; c) cheese grater.

⌂13) A creative blacksmith fashioned this: a) chimney cleaner; b) weapon; c) ham hook.

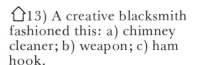

◁14) A spring loaded device to raise the lid of even the most heated situations.
L _ _ or P L _ T _
_ _ _ _ _ _

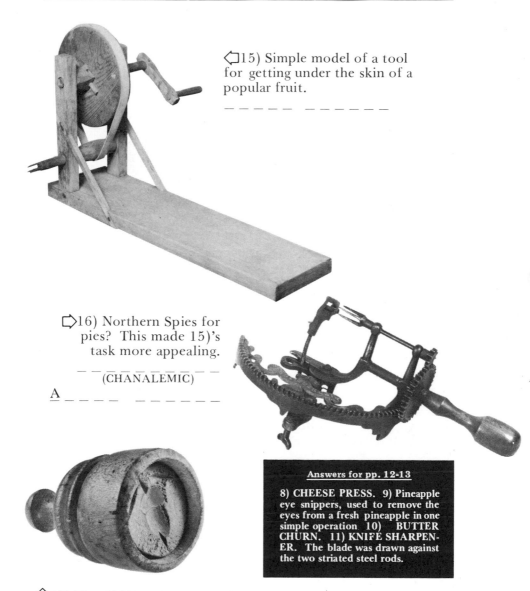

◁15) Simple model of a tool for getting under the skin of a popular fruit.

_ _ _ _ _   _ _ _ _ _

▷16) Northern Spies for pies? This made 15)'s task more appealing.

_ _ _ _ _ _ _ _ _ _ _
(CHANALEMIC)

A _ _ _ _   _ _ _ _ _

Answers for pp. 12-13

8) CHEESE PRESS. 9) Pineapple eye snippers, used to remove the eyes from a fresh pineapple in one simple operation 10)   BUTTER CHURN. 11) KNIFE SHARPEN-ER. The blade was drawn against the two striated steel rods.

⌂17) The 1897 Sears, Roebuck Catalogue featured an item very similar to this: a) hand-carved mouse trap; b) garlic press; c) butter mold; d) maple sugar stamp.

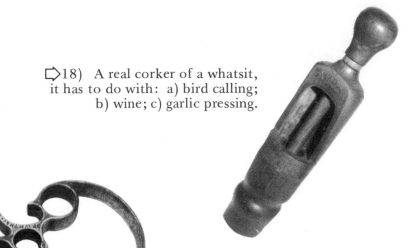

▷18) A real corker of a whatsit,
it has to do with: a) bird calling;
b) wine; c) garlic pressing.

◁19) A tool of many tasks,
it took on the hottest jobs
lying down.
T _ _ _ _ T

◁20) You plied these tongs and took
your lumps
To sweeten tea or when down in
the dumps.
S _ _ _ _ _ L _ _ _ _ _ _ _ _ E R

◁21) Clearly used for pouring: a) confections; b) decorations; c) candles; d) melted lead.

▷22) Not a small globe, but a: a) spherical grindstone; b) Van de Graaf generator; c) coffee bean roaster.

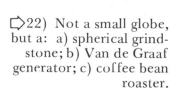

Answers for pp. 14-15

12) Apple slicer — apple was placed upon pin, pressed down upon blades; the core was pushed out the tube in the center. 13) Ham hook for hanging hams to smoke in chimney or smokehouse. 14) **LID OR PLATE LIFTER** for stove lids and hot plates. 15) Early wooden **APPLE PEELER.** 16) **MECHANICAL APPLE PEELER.** 17) Butter mold, used to stamp design on freshly made butter.

▷23) After the long pull was over, sweet tooths found this fancy little hammer handy.
_ _ _ _ _ B R _ _ _ _ R

◁24) Springboards to a popular German Christmas cookie.

‾ ‾(GERPRISLEN)‾ ‾
B _ _ _ _ S

⌂25) Might be an early sprayer, but is actually a: a) oil can; b) nursing bottle; c) watering can; d) tankard.

⌂26) Not a silver-plated moustache cup, this guaranteed warm, spoon-fed service at the Victorian dinner table. Whatsit? _ _ _ _ _
_ _ _ _ _

Answers for pp. 16-17

18) Wine—a bottle corker. Plunger was raised, cork placed in the opening. Device was put on top of bottle and plunger driven down, compressing the cork and forcing it into the bottle neck. 19) TRIVET, meat tenderizer, pot lifter, and household protector. 20) SUGAR LOAF BREAKER. 21) Candy ladle used by confectioners. 22) Coffee Bean Roaster. 23) TAFFY BREAKER, Enclosed in boxes of taffy to break it up into bite-sized pieces.

On the Farm

Life on the farm, too, was very different before the Age of Mechanization revolutionized the farmer's activities. A large part of the equipment required on the family farm was concerned with the management, care and use of the horse, the ox, and the mule. Animals, not the tractor and its multiform attachments (rivalling those of the modern sewing machine), were the farmer's principal source of energy, aside from the manpower and elbow grease exerted by himself and his helpers — often his children. The pace was slower and the yield smaller. It is helpful to keep these facts in mind when deducing the function of farm whatsits, here divided into three sections: ANIMAL, VEGETABLE, and MECHANICAL. Some are quite primitive, others of more sophisticated manufacture. Yet the efficiency of these old-time contrivances and the ingenuity displayed in their invention are considerable. Indeed, now that the one-family farm appears to be coming back in some areas of our country, many of these gadgets are in demand once more for actual use rather than as museum artifacts!

Animal

Every "whatsit" in this section has to do directly with the avian and apian, not to mention the bovine, porcine, and equine, members of the farm proletariat.

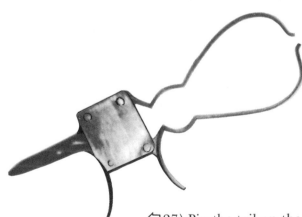

◁27) Pin the tail on the donkey? Not exactly, but therein lies a tail — of two legs, four legs and three legs.

_ _ _   _ _ I _   H _ _ _ _ R

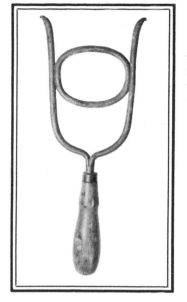

28) "Balling the jack" was the railroad term, but this balling jack was used to _____ when the vet came.

29) Keys are keys and
locks are locks;
These are keys to lock
an Ox.
Used to fasten ox _ _ _ _

30) Honey for jam. A launching pad for busy bees.

_ _ _ _ _ _ _ _ _ _

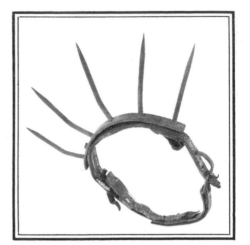

⇨ 31) A spiky little neck-
        lace to break the
             silver cord and
uncow the calf. Used for

_ _ _ _ _ _ _ _ _ _ _

⇧ 32) Gobble, gobble, how they hobble;
      Was a real art to drive this cart.
      (Essential for one of the fowler
          forms of transportation.)
      T _ _ _ _ Y Y _ _ _

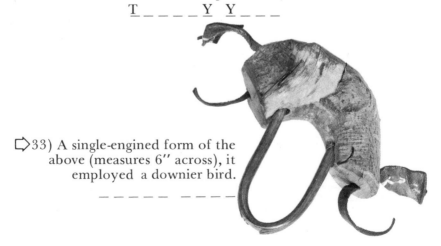

⇨ 33) A single-engined form of the
      above (measures 6″ across), it
          employed a downier bird.

      _ _ _ _ _ _ _ _ _

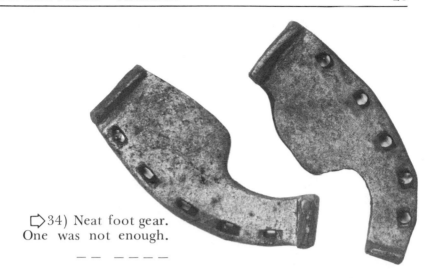

34) Neat foot gear.
One was not enough.

— — — — — —

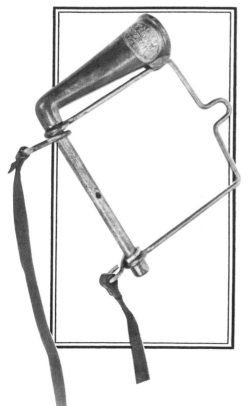

Answers for pp. 20-21

27) COW TAIL HOLDER; both
ends are spring-loaded clamps.
Large part encircles cow's back
leg, small jaws hold end of tail.
28) Hold open a horse's or cow's
mouth when administering physic
balls, removing objects from its
throat, or filing the teeth. 29)
BOWS. Made of both wood and
iron; wooden, whittled keys are
rare. 30) BEE BELLOWS. Used
by bee keepers to smoke bees
from the hive.

35) A doozey of a doser, to
make a stubborn mule take
his medicine. This device
buckled on to a _ _ _ _ _ _ _,
with the straight bar inserted
into the animal's _ _ _ _ _.

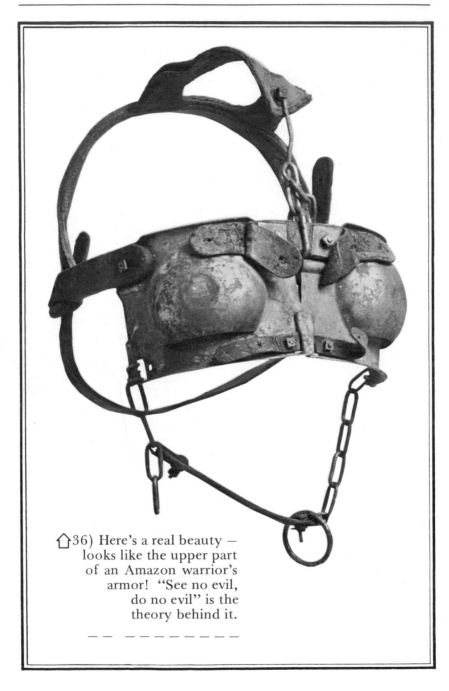

36) Here's a real beauty —
looks like the upper part
of an Amazon warrior's
armor! "See no evil,
do no evil" is the
theory behind it.

◁37) BOTTOMS UP!
Not an upside down
basket, this confined an
animal many times its
size — and on a diet.
_ X _ _ _ Z _ _

▷38) One's company, two's
a crowd, but not with
this device. Two
revolving spiked
wheels are separated by
a bar with a square
hole in the center.
_ _ _ _ _ W D _ _

▷ 39) To keep an ox off the
         vet's toes,
      These pincers clamped
         the animal's _____.
      Another invaluable aid
         to bovine medicare.

◁ 40) This odd-looking
apparatus was suspended
over a stanchion and
attached to the _____
of a young bull to
_____ them.

⬆ 41) You can lead a hog to slaughter,
       but you can't make him prink.
       The two words in this sentence
          that explain the function
          of this double-header are:

          _____ _____

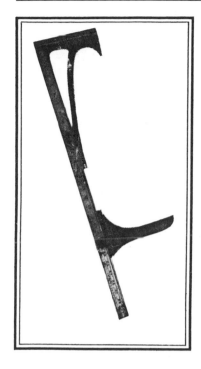

◁42) This old-fashioned

_ _ _ _ _ _ _
Measured collars for
a mammal.

Answers for pp. 24-25

36) OX BLINDERS. Placed over animal's eyes while it was being shod. The slits under the eye cups allowed the ox to see downwards. 37) OX MUZZLE. Extended crossbar at the base of the muzzle prevented ox from grazing. 38) OX CROWDER. Placed across the pole on an ox cart to keep the team from crowding.

▷43) In farriers' circles all
but duffers
Used to call this thing
a _ _ _ _ _ _ .
But another, name, more
descriptive of its function is

_ _ _ _ _ _ _   _ _ _ _ _ _
(LCCHIN)   (TRUCET)

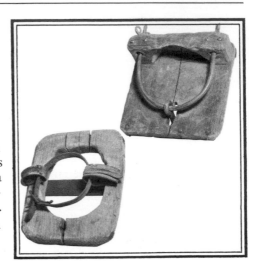

▷44) Clogs for bogs. A
necessity in the old days
for the harvest of a
distinctive sea-
side forage.
_ _ _ _ _ _ _ S

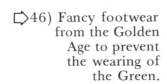

◁45) Along the main drag,
this _ _ _ _ _ _ _ _
was used to _ _ _ _ _ _ _ _.

▷46) Fancy footwear
from the Golden
Age to prevent
the wearing of
the Green.

_ _ _ _ _ _ _ _

◁ 47) This obsolete hoof cutter is called
a _ _ _ _ _ _ _ _

⌂ 48) A hot shot barber for the equine elite.

_ _ _ _ _ _ _ _   _ _ _ _ _
   (ENIGGINS)   (CHORT)

⌂ 49) Cold comfort for hoofers. This _ _ _ _
_ _ _ _ _ _ was used to prevent balling up.

Vegetable

Included herein are tools and appliances specifically designed for the planting, harvest, or processing of plants or plant products.

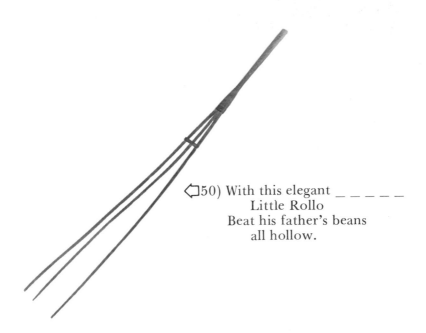

50) With this elegant _ _ _ _ _
Little Rollo
Beat his father's beans
all hollow.

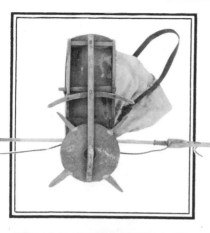

◁51) Strapped to his back, oh gentle reader,
The planter bore this

___ ___ _____

⬇52) No one wants to eat the Hull thing,
so these shoes stamped out the nuts in France.
They were used to

___ _____ ___

◁53) Linen stemmed from this device.

____ B_____

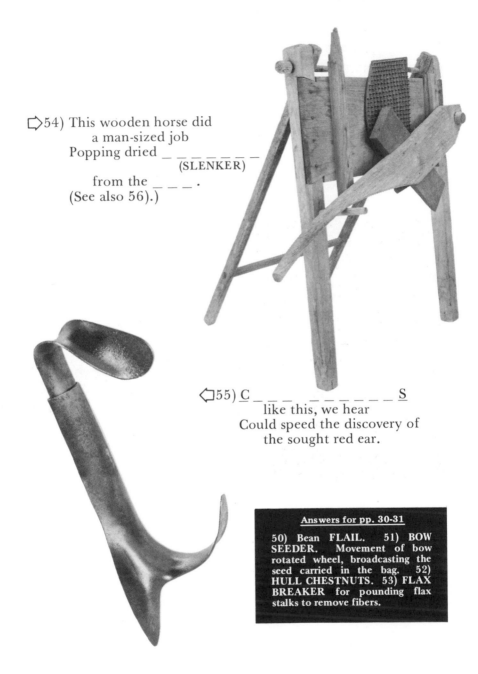

54) This wooden horse did
     a man-sized job
   Popping dried _ _ _ _ _ _ _
                 (SLENKER)
     from the _ _ _ .
   (See also 56).)

55) <u>C</u> _ _ _ _ _ _ _ _ _ <u>S</u>
       like this, we hear
   Could speed the discovery of
      the sought red ear.

56) In feeding stock, the

_ _ _ _
_ _ _ _ _ _ _
Was a welcome aid
to any feller.
(See also 54).)

⇨57) _ _ _ inside a mound
of _ _ _
To check condition
and decay.

⇦58) Drag these behind
your harrow
To plant your corn
straight and narrow.
F _ _ _ _ _   _ _ _ _ S

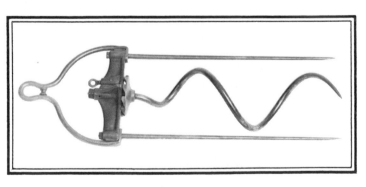

⇧59) Neither mole trap nor
post-hole digger,
This powerful tool hefted
something bigger.

_ _ _   _ _ _ _ _ _

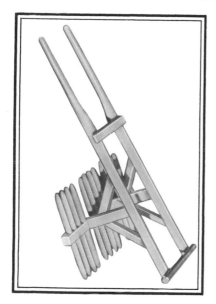

◁60) This horse-drawn harvesting device was probably the Granddaddy of a piece of mechanized equipment found on farms everywhere today.

– – –   – – – –

Answers for pp. 32-33

54) KERNELS, COB. Like 56), a corn sheller used to remove corn from cob for feeding livestock. 55) CORN HUSKERS. In an old-fashioned husking bee, anyone who found a red ear of corn under the husks got to kiss the person of his/her choice. 56) CORN SHELLER. The turning wheel activated movable grips that stripped the kernels from the cob.

◁61) Whatsit? a) long-handled cranberry scoop; b) apple grader; c) bean sifter; d) potato shovel.

◁62) Long-handled version of a harvesting tool much favored by antique buffs and decorators

_ _ _ _ _ _ _ _ _
_ _ _ _ _

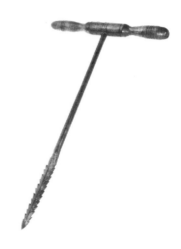

▷63) A needle for a haystack
or wool bale.
W _ _ _ or H _ _ _
_ _ _ _ _ _ _
(PRAMSEL)

⬆64) Multiple impressions
for the genus Allium.

_ _ _ _ _   _ _ _ _ _ _

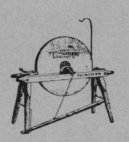

Mechanical

Under this category, we include tools and devices used on vehicles, for maintaining or fashioning farm equipment, and in woodworking and cutting.

◁ 65) Woodsman really had a
         blast —
       Lit a fuse and got out
         fast!
This is a _ _ _
_ _ _ _ T T _ _ _ _ _ _ _ _

66) Not a papoose
    frame, no joke;
    Used to shape
        _ _ _ _ for
    a _ _ _ _.

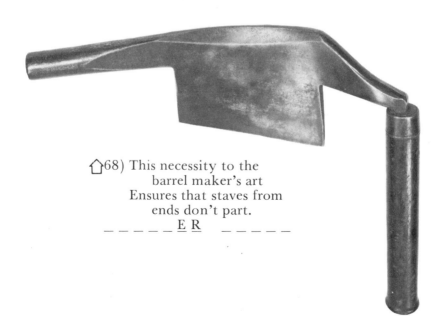

67) A real drag for big wheels. When the trail was all downhill, it helped to be on the skids.

_ _ _ _ _ _ _ _

68) This necessity to the
barrel maker's art
Ensures that staves from
ends don't part.
_ _ _ _ _ E R _ _ _ _ _

▷69) This crude but effective attachment had
a seasonal function. Under certain conditions,
it eased the user's burden considerably. It was
attached to a: a) block and tackle; b) ice skates;
c) wheelbarrow; d) sled runner; e) pung.

◁70) If the scythe was dull, he
wouldn't fret
Having on his belt the
means to _ _ _ _ .
(A wooden case for the
farmer's _ _ _ _ _ _ _ _ _)

▷71) This is a "twybil"
used by English fence makers.
What *is* a twybil?

_ _ _ _ _ _ _   _ _ _ _ _

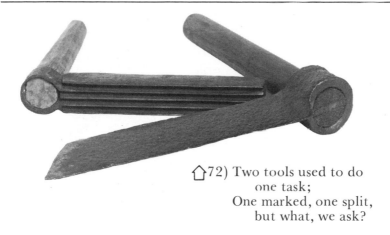

72) Two tools used to do
one task;
One marked, one split,
but what, we ask?

— — — — — — — —

73) A Teutonic blade for
the builder's trade.
It's an axe, all right,
but what kind?
a) headsman's axe;
b) double-bitted axe;
c) goosewing axe.

⇨74) A real Old-Timers' tool
used to _ _ _ _
the edge of a scythe
B _ _ _ _. (Hint—
its Lithuanian name
is something like
dengel stuck!)

⇦75) Bands or braces straighten
teeth in men;
This strange object S _ _ S
S _ _ teeth right again.

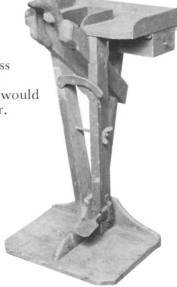

⇨76) To keep two harness
straps together,
A special _ _ _ _ would
hold the leather.

In the Home

What the tractor accomplished on the farm, electricity did for the home, providing heat, light, and power and executing in jig time all those tasks that used to require long hours of laborious handwork on the part of the housewife. Just think — back a while, before electricity, heat and hot water derived from stoves (you had to lug the water as well as the wood!); laundry was scrubbed piece by piece; ruffles and pleats had to be removed and reset at every washing; light was by fire, contained one way or another; and all clothing, blankets, and even rugs were produced by Mother's needle and busy fingers. The WHATSITS that follow conjure up in their own fashion the atmosphere of the old-time home and the challenges involved just in everyday living.

77) A spinning wheel?
No not quite —
The quill W _ _ _ _
Y _ _ _ right
up tight.

Answers for p. 42

74) PEEN, BLADE. Old-timers didn't sharpen a scythe with a stone or wheel. The edge of the blade was peened. The scyther sat on a slope with the cone-shaped piece of the dengel stuck imbedded in a block of wood held between his legs. The scythe was laid across this and the edge was peened with a hammer. This would make the metal harder as it was compressed, and the rippling effect would sharpen the blade. 75) SETS SAW. Patented saw-tooth set for two-man cross-cut saw.   76) VICE. The harness maker's vice considerably facili-tated harness repairs. Invaluable tool for large, horse-powered farms.

78) Not for angel cake
not yet for pies,
This handy gadget
catches _ _ _ _ _!

79) This early holder was
used to dandle
Light that came before
the candle.
_ _ _ _ _ _ _ _ _ _ holder.

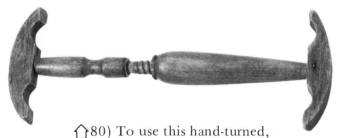

80) To use this hand-turned, adjustable wooden device, you would need a: a) spinning wheel; b) beaver hat; c) baby's rocker; d) yarn winder.

81) Yes, it's a churn, but only six inches high. It's meant not for milk but for

_ _ _ _ _ _ _ _ _ _ _ _ _ _.
(KNIFESHADERCH)

82) The laundress for the well-dressed lady or gentleman had to be skilled in the use of the _ _ _ _ _ _ _ _ _ _ _ _ _.

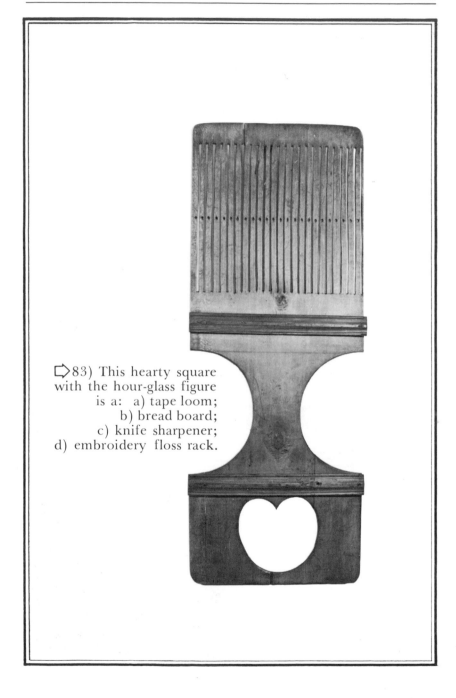

83) This hearty square
with the hour-glass figure
          is a: a) tape loom;
                     b) bread board;
             c) knife sharpener;
d) embroidery floss rack.

◁84) Never imprisoned in a
cage,
Mom's little bird was
quite the rage.
_ _ _ _ _ _   _ _ R D

▷85) For charcoal-grilled
shirts—a real flattener!
_ _ _ _   _ _ _ _

⌂86) The name of this sturdy
iron saucer dish derives
from the French word
graisse. It was called a
_ _ _ _ _ _ _, and
it was used to dip
_ _ _ _ _ for 79).

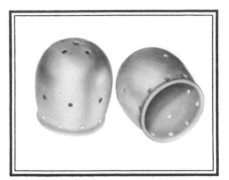

▷87) Boxing gloves? Not exactly—these digital covers for the crib crowd had a preventive function. They prevented _ _ _ _ _ _ _ _ _ _ _ _.

⌂88) A matchless hot foot for skiers, skaters, shovelers and all who yearn to fry with their boots on, this is fashioned of soapstone. Unscramble the letters to form the two-word definition.

‾ ‾‾ ‾‾ ‾‾ ‾ ‾‾ ‾‾ ‾‾ ‾ ‾
(BROWTERAMO)

Answers for pp. 46-47

83) Tape loom. Held between the knees while weaving tape. 84) SEWING BIRD was clamped to sewing table. The movable beak clasped material to keep it from the floor. The bird is equipped with a pincushion. 85) Charcoal burning FLAT IRON. Hot coals were inserted through trunk-like spout. 86) GRISSET, RUSHES. The dish held melted fat, into which the rush was dipped.

◁89) This hood-like attachment adapted kerosene lamps for use as a: a) letter-burner; b) dark lantern; c) invisible ink spotter; d) egg candler; e) projector.

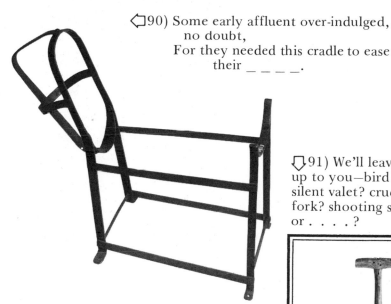

90) Some early affluent over-indulged,
no doubt,
For they needed this cradle to ease
their _ _ _ _.

91) We'll leave this one
up to you—bird perch?
silent valet? crude pitch-
fork? shooting stick?
or . . . . ?

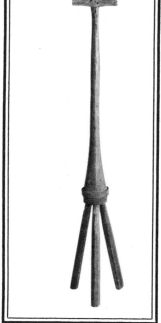

92)   Crackerjack!
For nuts on knees and not
on trees,
This armor plate was warm
and great.
From the clues above, can
you elicit
The double function of this
crazy whatsit?

1. _ _ _ _   _ _ _ _ _ _ _

2. _ _ _   _ _ _ _ _ _ _ _

⇧93) The lard pail set found this handle-and-strap contraption useful on the daily trek back and forth to school.

⇩94) When wet weather was afoot, this helped keep things warm and dry to boot. NOT a sadiron!

95) A cruelly effective form of mouth zipper. Used on 17th and 18th century scolds and called a _ _ _ _ _ _.

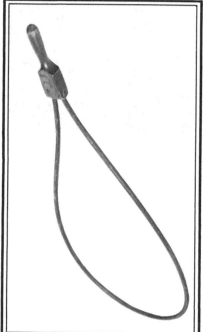

96) A wooden-handled rattan bow that really beat the Dutch—and Orientals too!

_ _ _   _ _ _ _ _ _

97) Used, we think, to reset what came out in the wash— a more sophisticated version of the doodad on page 45.

_ _ _ _ _ _ _

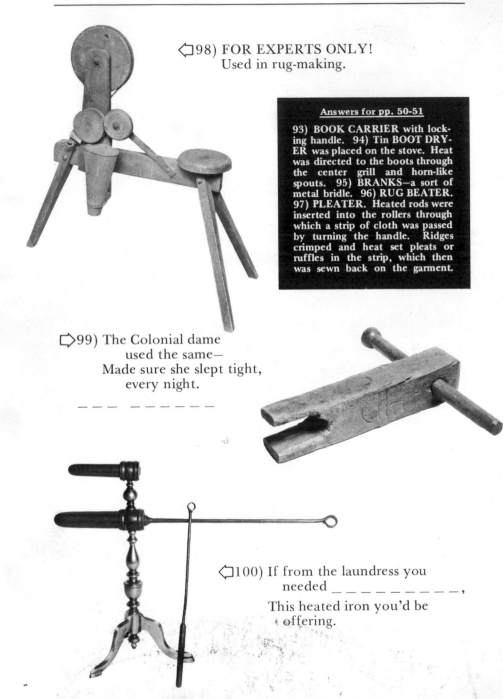

98) FOR EXPERTS ONLY!
Used in rug-making.

Answers for pp. 50-51

93) BOOK CARRIER with lock-
ing handle. 94) Tin BOOT DRY-
ER was placed on the stove. Heat
was directed to the boots through
the center grill and horn-like
spouts. 95) BRANKS—a sort of
metal bridle. 96) RUG BEATER.
97) PLEATER. Heated rods were
inserted into the rollers through
which a strip of cloth was passed
by turning the handle. Ridges
crimped and heat set pleats or
ruffles in the strip, which then
was sewn back on the garment.

99) The Colonial dame
used the same—
Made sure she slept tight,
every night.

___ _____

100) If from the laundress you
needed _ _ _ _ _ _ _ _ _,
This heated iron you'd be
offering.

Miscellaneous
and
Odd Bodikins

Containing assorted brain-teasers deriving from anywhere from the church to the railroads and back again. *Plus* a mystery page of whatsits still UNIDENTIFIED! If you know the identity of any of the objects on page 63, please write: Whatsit, Book Dept., Yankee, Inc., Dublin, N.H. 03444.

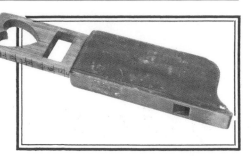

⇨101) For the choir master who wished to pitch in, this is a

_ _ _ _ _
_ _ _ _

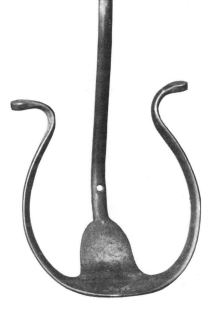

Answers for p. 52

98) Cylinder filling machine used for compressing rug filler material in loom cylinders.   99) BED WRENCH for tightening bed ropes on old-fashioned beds.   100) GOFFERING.   Material could be fluted (or de-fluted) by being drawn over the poker-heated tube.

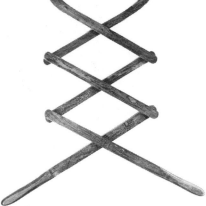

⇧102) A foothold to a settled yet traveling situation, these iron sconces served as

B_ _ _ _ _ _ _ _S

⇧103) Gate-like device used to deal with bestial church-goers that disturbed the service. Unscramble the anagram to find the two-word definition.

_ _ _ _ _ _ _ _ _
(GGONTSOD)

104) This held something, there is no doubt. But what? a) logs; b) clay pipes; or c) a foot with gout.

105) Where restraint was called for, but not self-applied, This served the purpose, the miscreant inside.

_ _ _ T R _ _ _ _ I N G
_ _ _ _

106) For the parishioner sitting through sermons long and dreary, 'Twas a rest of sorts for a limb most weary.

_ _ _ _ _ S T

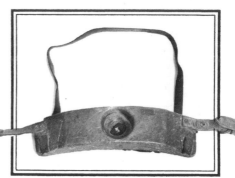

▷107) A most intriguing
arrangement, obviously a:
a) flag-holding harness;
b) magnifying eye-piece for
a cyclops; c) chairmaker's
harness; d) donkey harness.

◁108) For the craftsman, this
tool when skillfully
applied
Made sitting on one's
work easier on the
bottom side.
_ _ _ _ _ or _ _ _ _ _ E R

▷109) In an age of grace in dress,
manners, and mode
of travel,
This protected the first, when
mounting the last, from
mud and gravel.
_ _ G G _ W _ _ _ _ _ _ _ R

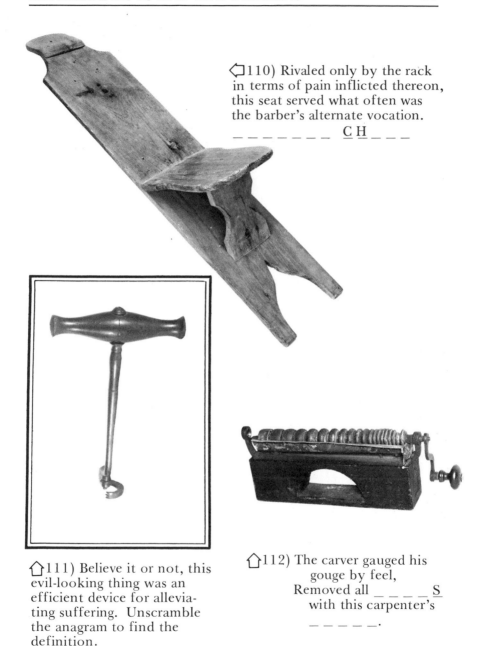

110) Rivaled only by the rack in terms of pain inflicted thereon, this seat served what often was the barber's alternate vocation.

_ _ _ _ _ _ _ C H _ _ _

111) Believe it or not, this evil-looking thing was an efficient device for alleviating suffering. Unscramble the anagram to find the definition.

_ _ _ _ _ _ _ _ _ _ _ _ _

(HOTTO)   (CRAXTORTE)

112) The carver gauged his gouge by feel, Removed all _ _ _ _ S with this carpenter's

_ _ _ _ _.

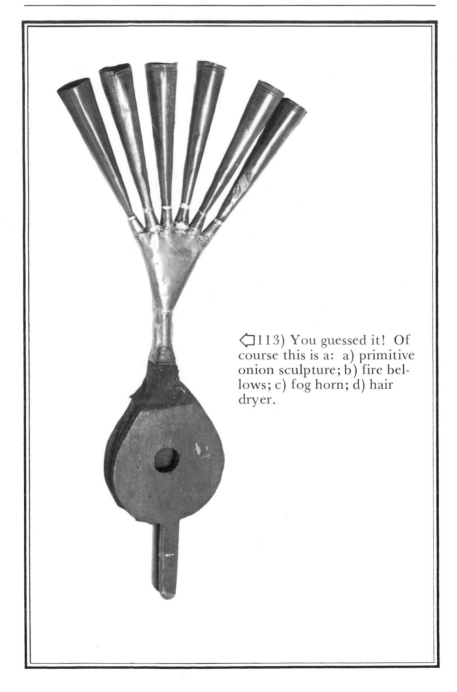

113) You guessed it! Of course this is a: a) primitive onion sculpture; b) fire bellows; c) fog horn; d) hair dryer.

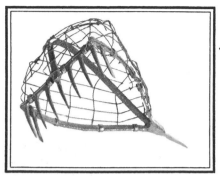

114) A rake that handled right
       eased the task it
    Is to put _ _ _ _ _ really
    in the basket.

115) A special used by
       fisherpeople
    Who wove _ _ _
       _ _ _ _ s
    about its steeple.

116) The spiky object
pictured right was used by:
a) blacksmiths; b) people with
itchy backs; c) fishermen;
d) gardeners; e) housewives.

▷117) Not a tooth extractor, this whatsit gave tooth to a popular weapon. Note the cutting blades activated by the handle.
M _ _ _ _ _ _ _ L L
        M _ _ _

◁118)   ,
A _ _ _ _ _ _ _ '_ _ _ _ _ was required to make a whole barrel of monkeys — or anything else.

Answers for pp. 58-59

113) A fog horn worked by bellows. 114) CLAMS. A clam rake. Original long handle has broken off. 115) EEL TRAPS. Fishermen wove stripped willow or similar material over this eel trap mold to construct a basket-like device for trapping eels. 116) Fishermen. It is a fishing cresset. Spiky portion held flaming pine knots; lighted, the cresset was held out over the boat at night to attract fish — particularly shad.

⌂119) This has to do with tires, iron, Put by a blacksmith on a wagon.
It is a _ _ _ _ _ _ _ _ _
        (E A R L V E R T)

⌂120) This elongated hammer with a slight whip to its handle was used by a: a) blacksmith; b) cooper; c) whipmaker; d) wheelwright; e) reeve.

121) This gadget belongs to the Age of Railroads,when it was a familiar sight; today, its function is not easy to deduce.

P _ _ _ _ _ N C _ _
_ _ _ _ _ _ J _ _ _

122) Here's an item that baffled the experts. The name "Winterking" is recognizable on the top. The adjustable opening between the two side plates, and covered flue, suggests a portable charcoal-burning heater. Can *you* solve the mystery? (Hint: It too has a railroad connection.)

123) An odd-looking contraption that made for light work at the cobbler's bench.

_ _ _ _ _ _ _ 'S
_ _ _ _ _

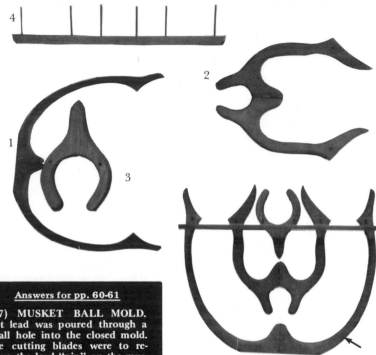

⬆124) The riddle posed by
this hard-wood thingamajig
discovered in Ontario, Canada,
was solved by an Ohio
Yankee reader who grew up in
Ontario around the turn
of the century.
Four pieces: 1) and 2) are
each hinged to fold in half.
3) does not fold and is
positioned in reverse in
assembled photo (arrow). 4) a
bar with 6 metal rods that
fit into holes at each end
of pieces 1), 2) and 3).
WHATSIT?

(See page 10 for answer.)

and finally . . . here are some MYSTERIES . . . as yet unresolved. If *you* know what they are, please write and tell us!

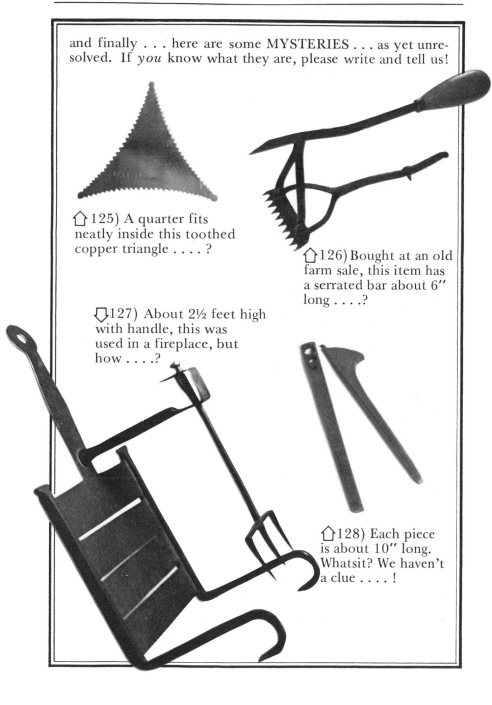

⌂ 125) A quarter fits neatly inside this toothed copper triangle . . . . ?

⌂ 126) Bought at an old farm sale, this item has a serrated bar about 6″ long . . . . ?

⬇127) About 2½ feet high with handle, this was used in a fireplace, but how . . . . ?

⌂ 128) Each piece is about 10″ long. Whatsit? We haven't a clue . . . . !

Index

Each item is followed by its number in the book and the page on which it appears, in that order.